CHRISTMAS PLAYS
FROM
OBERUFER

THE PARADISE PLAY
THE SHEPHERDS' PLAY
THE THREE KINGS' PLAY

Translated by A. C. HARWOOD

GW00670923

Rudolf Steiner Press
London

First edition in English 1944
Second edition 1961
Third edition 1973

To the First Actors of these plays in England—
The Teachers of Michael Hall

ISBN 0 85440 279 9

MADE AND PRINTED IN GREAT BRITAIN BY
THE GARDEN CITY PRESS LIMITED
LETCHWORTH, HERTFORDSHIRE
SG6 1JS

PREFACE

The Plays here translated were collected in the forties of last century by Karl Julius Schröer—the friend and teacher of Rudolf Steiner—from the little island of Oberufer on the Danube near Pressburg, close to the frontiers of Austria and Hungary. Some time in the sixteenth or early seventeenth century a group of German people had migrated there from the neighbourhood of Lake Constance and had taken with them the cycle of religious plays which they had received by tradition from their ancestors. When Schröer collected the plays, the parts were still hereditary in certain families; no complete copy existed but each family treasured a manuscript of the words of one particular part. Surrounded as they were by people of a different nation and speaking a different language, the peasants of Oberufer preserved unaltered, in a way found in no other similar German plays, both the text itself and the tradition of acting.

The preparation for the Plays and the manner of acting have been thus described by Rudolf Steiner, who received the account from Schröer himself. In the Autumn, after harvest, the peasants who were to take part met together and rehearsals began. All parts were played by men, as in the Elizabethan theatre, and during the time of rehearsal all members of the caste had to lead—as far as they could—a moral and respectable life, abstaining alike from visits to alehouses and from the singing of bawdy songs. Before the actual performance the whole company went in procession through the village. They were headed by the 'Tree-singer', who carried in his hand the small 'Paradise Tree'—a kind of symbol of the Tree of Life—and the rear was brought up by the 'Star singer', who bore a golden star on the end of multiple wooden scissors—a larger version of a familiar children's toy—which could shoot the star

3

over the other actors and hold it aloft over the head of Mary. On reaching the inn where the performance was to take place, the company went in to dress, with the exception of the Angel, who stayed outside, and the Devil, who ran riot through the town, blowing a cowhorn and driving everyone he could into the inn to see the performance. Once in the inn the audience arranged itself in a horse-shoe and the performance began, the Tree-singer acting as prologue to the Paradise, and the Star-singer to the Shepherds' Play. After these two plays, of which the Paradise play was acted second, a third satirical comedy—somewhat in the Greek fashion—was added, in which, however, the actors who had played the Holy Characters were not allowed to take part. The Play of the Three Kings was acted at another time and under somewhat different circumstances, being in closer connection with the church. The Paradise and Shepherds' Nativity Play, however, were always associated together; for in the Middle Ages they still knew, what modern man has forgotten, that there is no meaning in the Redemption without the Fall, and that

> 'Had not the apple taken been
> The apple taken been
> Then had never our Lady,
> A-been Heaven's Queen.'

The form of the Plays seems to point to the very origin of drama. The actors, or singers as they were called, sing a song in procession, after which the characters concerned come forward and act what has just been sung, while the rest of the company seat themselves at the back or side of the stage. This ancient form is especially marked in the case of the Paradise Play, which is really one long ballad interspersed with dramatic scenes. The Devil acts as scene-shifter in the Paradise Play; and the Devil for Herod, and the Page for the Kings in the Three Kings' Play. Traditionally, the Angel in the Shepherds' Play carries a star on a staff, and the Angel in the Kings' Play has a picture of Mother and Child beneath the star.

A word may be added about the translation. When

there is much wonderful poetry in such old English Plays as the Coventry Plays, it may seem superfluous to translate Christmas Plays from another tongue. Experience has shown, however, that these particular plays, which are both more childlike and more dramatic than the old English plays, make a deeper impression on children than any other old plays available. For a dreadful alternative waits on the would-be-writer of modern Nativity Plays. To make the thing realistic, and convince the audience that it really did happen, and a real baby was born in a real stable, he has to introduce language from a life with so different an idiom that it falsifies the picture of the birth of a child in an age when the bearing of children was treated both more simply and more spiritually than it is today. Or he may treat the theme poetically, with the almost inevitable consequence of reducing the matter to a beautiful dream, in which idealized shepherds salute a symbolic child. The life of the Middle Ages, however, was still sufficiently akin to the time of the Birth of Christ for the Nativity to be represented in its own language and forms.

The original plays are in dialect and lose enormously in vigour and colour in any non-dialect translation. Unfortunately most modern English people have been robbed of their birth-right of a dialect, and, being myself one of those unfortunates, I have been forced to put the translation into a kind of biblical English with some deliberate archaisms. I hope that readers will find the language on the right side of Wardour Street. But the plays are not meant to be read, and in actual performance the translation has stood the test of a good many annual performances. The two prologues probably form the least satisfactory part. They can either be omitted, or provide the basis for such local pleasantries as may suit the particular performance.

The music composed by Leopold van der Pals on the basis of the original folk melodies may be procured through the publishers of this translation.

For this English version music has also been composed by Mr Brian Masters, to whom enquiries should be addressed at Michael Hall, Forest Row, Sussex.   A.C.H.

THE PARADISE PLAY

The Tree-Singer's Prologue

Come, players and singers, rejoice and be glad,
I tell you great honour this day you have had,
The whole worshipful town is gathered today
To hear your singing and mark your play.
So heartily, lads; each tune sing true,
And show these good folk what you can do.
Put on your best faces; let each word tell;
And sound me your notes as clear as a bell.
But first your greeting to one and all,
Together assembled in this hall.

Come, greet me the Father on his high throne,
And greet me his only begotten Son,
Greet me the Holy Spirit also
That he lead our Souls the way we should go,
And greet both Father and Spirit and Son,
Most Holy Trinity, Three in One.
Greet Adam and Eva, and each bird and beast
In Paradise here, both greatest and least.
And greet me the firmament that God's hand
Did make at the end of the world for to stand.
Our parish as well we must never forget,
So greet we its Council and all of their set,
And the one above all who sits in the Chair,
Come greet him—God's will must have put him
    there.
And now, my good singers, strike up again,
And greet yonder tree with a lusty refrain:
Of the fruit of that tree man never should eat,
If so be he'd keep a right watch on his feet.
So greet me the tree, that of all bears the crown,
And likewise the apples that from it hang down.
But O, that wretch Eva she ate of the fruit,
And with her that booby called Adam to boot,
So God cast them out for the sin of their deed
Of which in our hearts we should ever take heed.
For the Devil alone our greeting shall fail—

7

May God keep us from him. Let's all pull his tail.
And now, my good singers, when Adam fell
How all things were changed, you know it right
    well:
So last greet our master, the bravest of hearts,
God bless him, who taught us our cues and our
    parts,
And gave us the will to go through with our play.
Dear singers, your old friend has no more to say.

The Company Sing as They Enter

O let me enter in this place
To sing with my heart's might,
And grant my mouth, O Lord, the grace
To sound thy praise aright.
In simple truth I rede
Thou art my God indeed;
Thou hast withouten aid
All things and creatures made.
Praise God for evermore!

But see, but see a tree stands here
Which precious fruit doth bear,
That God has made his firm decree
It shall not eaten be,
Yea, rind and flesh and stone
We shall leave well alone.
This tree is very life,
Therefore God will not have
That man shall eat thereof.

Enter the Angel Gabriel

In right good faith I enter this place.
God give you Good Evening of his grace,
A right good evening, the best of cheer,
The Lord of Heaven grant each man here.
Most reverent Worships, both Master and Dame,
Our service. To you, pretty maidens, the same.
We shall but trouble you, by your leave,
While here of Adam and of Eve
Their woeful sin we shall you show,
From Paradise they needs must go,—
So silence, gentles all, we pray,
And grant your hearts to hear our play.

The Company Sing

How fresh the morning doth appear,
Before the sunrise we are here,
To God on his throne,
Our praise we make known.

From Babylon we took our leave
To sing you all this joyful stave,
     To God, etc.

As God did in his Godhead brood
He made the world and saw 'twas good,
     To God, etc.

Yea, beastes all both small and great,
And living man he did create,
     To God, etc.

In the beginning God did found
The earth, and made the welkin round,
     To God, etc.

He made the firmament also,
And two great lights therein to show,
     To God, etc.

The one is day, the other night,
For God hath made them both aright,
     To God, etc.

He Adam made by his great skill
And set in Paradise to dwell,
     To God, etc.

The Lord God Speaks

Adam, the living breath essay
I give thee with this light of day,
And reason that thou know thy God
Hath formed thee living from the sod.
But time it is thy life began,
Stand on thy feet and be a man.
Say, Adam, how the world doth strike thee?—
All fresh and shining—doth it like thee?
The earth with all its brave adorning,

9

The sunshine of this first bright morning,
The firmament majestical,
What, Adam, art thou pleased withal?
Speak, man, I yearn to know thy mind.

Adam Speaks

O Father, very good I find
What in thy Godhead thou hast made,
My strength is in my wisdom stayed,
My good to do thy holy will,
For thou hast made and keepest me still,
In me thine image is revealed.

The Lord God Speaks

Take thou the creatures of the field,
Adam, to thee they are assigned
To do thee service in their kind.
The earth with hills and mountains steep
I give thee, fishes of the deep
And birds of air, that by this hand
I made, I give to thy command.
Share thou with me my domination,
And be the lord of all creation.
On thee a garden I bestow,
Master of all the trees that grow,
Whose branches with ripe fruit are bent
Which thou may'st eat to thy content.
One sole command (the rest is free)
I give thee now. Look on this tree
Of good and evil, that doth stand
Hard in the midst of this fair land,
For that of trees it is most sweet,—
Of this alone thou shalt not eat,
But shouldst thou shameless prove and proud,
And eat of this tree disallowed,
Then shalt thou perish in a breath
And die an everlasting death.
Whereby thou knowest thy God am I,
Who make to live and make to die;
Yea, life and death as I ordain
I give, and I can take again.

The Company Sing

Adam, thy Creator know,

Who doth all things on thee bestow,
To God on his throne
Our praise we make known.

He gave the goodly fruits of earth
That thou might'st live withouten dearth,
        To God, etc.

One tree he set aside of all,
That into harm thou might'st not fall,
        To God, etc.

Knowledge it is of evil and good;
God spake it: write it in thy blood.
        To God, etc.

God did cause a slumber deep
To fall on Adam, and he did sleep,
        To God, etc.

He took a rib from Adam's side,
And made a woman to be his bride.
        To God, etc.

The Lord God Speaks

I took a rib from Adam's side
And made a woman to be his bride;
Adam, awake and stand upright,
Behold thy equal come to light.
Formed she is from out thy side
To be thy helpmeet and thy bride,
Formed she is from out thy bone,
Wherefore cleave thou to her alone.
My angel shall protect your ways,
My blessing be on all your days,
Be fruitful, multiply, fill the earth,
Ye shall have plenty withouten dearth,
Be but obedient to my word.

Adam Speaks

Yea, that will I right well, O Lord,
And here receive what thou doest give,
All creatures, and myself to live.
Look, Eva, in what happy wise

11

We here may live in Paradise;
God hath for us this garden set,
To dwell there without toil or sweat;
One sole command we must obey,
The Lord hath laid on us this day.
But listen how the small birds sing,
And see the beastes leap and spring!
What goodly trees the Lord hath made,
With leafy boughs to give us shade,
And fruit that we may freely share.—
Only one tree we must forbear,
Midmost it stands, it is the best,
But of its fruit we must not taste;
For should we shameless prove and proud
And eat the tree He disallowed,
Then shall we perish in a breath
And die an everlasting death.
Whereby we know He is our God
Who made us living from the sod,
Yea, life and death, as he ordain,
He gives and He can take again.

Company Sing

Now are they filled with joy and bliss,
All things are framed to their service,
To God on his throne
Our praise we make known.

Of which the Devil straight is ware,
And secretly he creepeth there,
  To God, etc.

Yea, in a serpent's guise
Dwelt there in Paradise.
  To God, etc.

The Devil Speaks

Here creep I into Paradise,
Gliding in a serpent's guise,
God hath created a woman and man
And finished them off all spick and span
And set them in his house and hall,
But I'll soon see them over the wall.
Therefore to Paradise I came up,

12

And put it in their mind to sup.
Now wherefore may they to their mind
Eat of fruit of every kind,
But this one tree, which is most sweet,
Of this alone they may not eat?
Adam, this fruit if thou wilt take,
Thou mayest be thy Lordes make;
Eva, this apple take, as right
Thine own heart gives thee appetite,
And give to Adam that he bite.

Company Sing

An apple from the bough he brake,
Gave to Eva and she ate.
To God on his throne
Our praise we make known.

Eva Speaks

Adam, sith man and wife we be,
I pray thee, look on yonder tree,
Whereon such lovely fruits abound,
The like of them I never found,
Now to taste it give me leave;

She Bites the Apple

As I am an honest Eve,
It is heart's good to eat thereof,
Adam, an thou do me love,
Take and bite it in all haste,
It hath so wonderful a taste.

Adam Speaks

If of this apple I do eat
It is that thou dost me entreat;
I eat not of my will alone.

He Eats of the Apple

Ah, how my soul is overthrown!

Company Sing

Adam on that apple fed,
And his eyes were opened,
        To God, etc.
And when he ate it, in that hour

All the world was wounded sore.
    To God, etc.

The Devil Speaks

I am the Devil of wedded folk,
Well known to all who bear that yoke,
What sense they have they get from me,
Which is not more than it needs to be.
The man shall hang himself for his trouble,
The woman shall drown herself, bubble, bubble,
A Martyr's crown will fit them well,
And they'll get their grave with me in Hell.
Adam and Eve I have so cheated
And by my cunning so entreated
That God's command they have set aside,
And eaten what the Lord denied.
Good end to vermin such as they,
O what a marvellous trick to play!—
I don't for nothing give apples away.
If Adam and Eve had eat plum-cake
They wouldn't have caught such a belly-ache.

Adam Speaks

Ah, how my soul is overthrown!
O wife, I have great evil done,
That I have hearkened unto thee.
A naked sword aloft I see,
And naked all and stark am I,
O wife, we have sinned grievously!

God Speaks

Where are thou, Adam? Come here to me.

Adam Speaks

O Lord, here am I,
Before thine eyes I am ashamed.

The Lord God Speaks

Why art thou ashamed?

Adam Speaks

For that thy covenant I have slighted.

The Lord God Speaks

Thinkest thou it shall go unrequited,

14

When one tree only I forbade thee?
Say, who did unto this persuade thee?

Adam Speaks

Ah, Lord, I swear it on my life,
Eve, whom thou gavest me to wife,
She took the fruit and gave to me.
Would God that I had let it be.
She brake an apple from the bough,
And bit therein, and showed me how,
And brake in that same hour thy word,
E'en as thou camest hither, Lord.

The Lord God Speaks

Where is thy wife? Show her to me.

Adam Speaks

Here, Lord, she stands, beneath the tree.

The Lord God Speaks

Eva, say on. What hast thou done?

Eva Speaks

Ah, Lord, the snake did so persuade
I took the fruit thou hadst forbade,
And gave to Adam of my store,
Ah Lord, we will not do it more!

The Lord God Speaks

Angel Gabriel, come hither to me.
This naked sword I give to thee,
That therewith Adam and Eva wise
Thou drive them out of Paradise,
And by my glory, power, honour,
They come within it nevermore.

Company Sing

There came an angel with flaming sword,
And drove them forth before the Lord.
    To God, etc.

The Angel Speaks ②

Lo, a command most sure have I

15

Received from God, the Lord Most High,
That Adam now and Eva wise
I drive them forth from Paradise,
From Paradise you needs must go,
To till the soil with labour slow.
Adam, thou in fear and dread
With thy brow's sweat shalt win thy bread;
Eva, for thou this fruit hast ta'en,
Shalt bring forth children with great pain.

Eva Speaks

Alas, poor womankind, that I
Should bring them to this misery.
But sith 'tis so, we must be bold
Ourselves subject to God to hold,
And keep in all things His decree.

Adam Speaks

My dearest wife, come here to me,
Not long, not long, Lord, I implore,
But call us quickly home once more.

The Angel Speaks

Out of this place together go,
I shall recall you late and slow.

Eva Speaks

My God, forsake me not I pray!

The Angel Speaks

Eva, cast thou thy doubts away,
Cleave to thy husband, thy children tend,
So God forgive thee at the end.

The Company Sing

Adam thus and Eva wise
Are driven out of Paradise.
     To God, etc.

The Devil Speaks

I have beguiled this precious pair
And out of Paradise lied them fair;
But trust me for an eye to find them,
And chains to snap and straitly bind them.

16

* *

Lord Ruler, I cry Murder, Haroo,
On Adam and Eve, these culprits two,
Who thy commandment, Sire, have slighted,—
I know it shall not be unrequited.
They've fallen into the world of sin,
Where trouble's always creeping in;
And there I'm mostly to be found,
Looking about me and puffing around,
With a rant and roar I arrive pell-mell—
It isn't exactly quiet in Hell.
I'll blow the fires to a gentle heat,
And, Lord, how Adam and Eve shall sweat!
I'll bind them for Thee with iron bands,
And none shall snatch them out of my hands.

The Lord God Speaks

Get thee gone, Satan, thou hound of Hell,
Knowest thou not what a shameful word thy lips
    have let fall!

Satan Falls

The dust of the earth shall be thy food,
And on thy belly thou shalt crawl
Against the use of beastes all.
See now, this Adam such wealth has won
Like to a God he is become,
Knowledge he has of evil and good,
He can lift up his hand on high,
Whereby he liveth eternally.

The Company Sing as They Go Out

O Holy Trinity,
O Godlike Sovereignty,
Who Death and the fiend and Hell,
By your great might did quell,
And unto us do give
Eternal life to live,
We praise you evermore,
He who can read our mind
Grant us his Realm to find.

The Angel Speaks

Most reverent Worships, both Master and Dame,
Our service. To you, pretty maidens, the same,

17

I come but to say, now all is ended
We trust that in naught we have offended.
We have but shown Almighty God
He hath made all, and from the sod
Adam in stark and naked state
In his own image did create;
But the snake so tempted Adam and Eve
That God's commandment they did leave
On fruit which he forbad to feed,
Whereby they fell in fear and need,
And everlasting death to end,
Till of his mercy God did send
His Son, who is his Son alone,
For sin of man to make atone.
So think no evil, nor chide our play,
But if in aught we have gone astray
And shown your Worships what was not fit,
Blame not our will, but our lack of wit,
Show we have pleased, so all's made right—
And we wish you from God Almighty, **Good
Night.**

* * *

THE SHEPHERDS' PLAY

The Star-Singer Speaks

Come, gather round me, my merry choir,
Like chestnuts roasting round the fire.
Spread yourselves, Masters. Fill your lungs—
But ere you sing your lusty songs,
In God's name greet me one and all,
And on the Trinity first we call.
God bless the Holy Ghost; God bless the Son;
God bless God himself on his heavenly throne;
God bless them as three; and God bless them as
one.
God bless goodman Joseph, and Mary his spouse,
And God bless the stable that stood them for
house.

18

And God bless the child that was born in the
  stable.
And the ox and the ass that stood by his cradle.
God bless sun and moon and the stars of the night,
And God bless the darkness that makes them so
  bright.
And the grass, and the dew on the grass, and the
  weather,
God bless it, that wets you and us, Sirs, together.
God bless the Queen with her sceptre and crown,
And God bless his Worship, the Mayor of this
  town.
And now, my fine singers, this way turn your
  hands
And greet me the star, and the stick where it
  stands,
And greet the star-scissors, though nothing they cut,
God bless them open—and God bless them shut:
And the bolts and the bars, so stout and so strong,
God bless them that carry the brave star along.
And our master, who learned every player his
  part,
Until (by God's grace) we had got them by heart,
Come, greet him. And greet all good folk in this
  hall.
And end me your greetings with God bless us all.

The Company Sing

Bless, O Lord, the way we tread,
Bless our coming and our going;
Bless likewise our daily bread,
Bless our leaving and our doing,
Bless our death with thy death's leaven
That to us thy life be given.

The Angel Speaks |

In right good faith I enter this place,
God give you good evening of his grace,
A right good evening, the best of cheer,
The Lord of Heaven grant each man here.
Most reverent Worships, both Master and Dame,
Our service. To you, pretty maidens, the same.
Pray of your courtesy this day
For one brief hour to mark our play.

We bring you here no heathen tale,
Nor things men gossip o'er their ale,
Which for your Worships were all unfit,
But all is ta'en from Holy Writ;
Namely of Christ and Christes birth,
Who for our help was man on earth.
So silence, goodmen all, we pray
And grant your hearts to hear our play.

The Company March Round and Sing

When God the Almighty Lord
Would keep his promised word,
All for that blessed end
His Angel he did send,
And Gabriel his name.
Unto Nazareth he came
And Mary on that day
Saluted with Ave,
Who was unto her own
Betrothed man unknown.

*The Angel Gabriel Enters, Stands Before Mary and
Speaks*

Gabriel 2 Robert.

Hail, thou gracious one,
God the Lord is with thee,
Blessed art though amongst women.
Behold thou shalt conceive,
And bring forth a son,
And shalt call his name Jesus—
And he shall be a Lord over his folk for ever.

Mary

How shall this be,
Seeing I know not a man?

Angel 2

Behold, I am the angel Gabriel
That proclaim it unto thee.
The Holy Ghost shall come upon thee,
And the power of the Highest shall overshadow
    thee,

20

Therefore also that holy thing which shall be born
   of thee
Shall be called the Son of God;
And behold thy cousin Elizabeth
She hath conceived a son in her old age,
And this is now the sixth month with her
Whose reproach it was to be called barren.
For with God all things are possible.

Mary

Lo, I am the Lord's handmaid.
May it come to pass with me as thou hast said.

The Angel Goes Out, Mary Stays. The Company
Form Their Procession and Mary Joins Them

All Sing

So while Mary is with child
In Augustus' day,
See the prophecy fulfilled
No man can gainsay.
Caesar sendeth forth decree
All the folk shall taxed be
In their number truly,
Now upon the appointed morn
To the place where they were born
All betake them duly.

Repeat,   *All Go Off, Only Mary and Joseph Staying.*

Joseph Speaks

Caesar Augustus has made decree
All the world shall taxed be,
On every house the tribute laid
Straight and strictly must be paid,
Or all its goods shall forfeit be.
Ah God, what will become of me?
What shall I do? Where shall I turn?
My daily bread I scarce can earn.
My shaky hand and dimming eye
No more avail my craft to ply,
And all I have, my little store,
Scarce keeps the wolf from out the door.

21

Yet needs I must the tribute pay
And Caesar's dread decree obey.

Mary

Ah, Joseph, be not in such fear,
Certain some good man dwelling near
Will give us help and timely rede
And lend us money in our need.

Joseph

And pray where is the neighbour friend
That has so great a sum to lend?
Look you for gold on every tree?
Nay, wife, talk not vain hopes to me.

Mary

Husband, one thing is left us still
Whereby to do Augustus' will.
Come, let us drive our ox to town,
And when to Bethlehem we come down,
Sell him at market as best we may,
And so get money the tax to pay.

Joseph

Without our ox how shall we stead?
Where shall we look for daily bread?
As well might Caesar take life and blood
As the beast that gains our livelihood.
Yet all you say and more must we do
I doubt the ox will pay for two.
Take we the ass—on him you may ride,
And I with the ox will journey beside.

The Company Sing

Great Caesar from his royal throne
Hath spoken: that his will be done.
Take tribute, ride from town and shire,
Bring gold and goods to his desire.

Joseph is risen and gone down
With Mary to the taxing town,
Who straightway as the journey's done
In Bethlehem bringeth forth her son.

They Begin Their Journey

Mary

But in the crowded city's wall
Where shall our cattle find a stall?

Joseph

I know an innkeeper, by name
Rufinus, and my friend—the same
Shall ease us well with bite and sup
And put our weary cattle up.

Mary

But how if others come before
And house be full, and they shut the door?
For many the folk, both young and old,
That ride to the taxing when all must be told.

Joseph

Fear not; the town lies here before
Come, let us prick our beasts the more,
Lest doors be barred and folk abed,
And on cold stones we rest our head.

Mary

Ah Joseph be not in such haste
Too heavy am I to go so fast.
The way with ice is coated o'er
To slip and fall I tremble sore,
My limbs with cold are numb and dead,
And of some evil I have great dread.

Joseph

This evening you shall warm them through
By good inn fire, I promise you.
For see, before the house I stand,
And shall my friend's good help command.

He Knocks at the Door

Rufinus, my friend, now welcome us right,—
Hast thou not lodging for us this night?
Needs not to say, what thou well canst see,
Full weary we come from a far journey.

Hard in our face the North did blow,
And battered us sore with ice and snow.

First Innkeeper, Rufinus

My friend you must apply next door,
My house is packed from roof to floor.
You're not the first—this very day
I've turned them by the score away.
I'm Master of this Hostelry
And order my house in my degree.

Joseph

Alas, this was my only friend,
Except the Lord some other send.
Come, let us try our luck elsewhere—
A good heart never knows despair.
The neighbouring host we'll kindly greet,
And call for lodging, drink and meat.

He Knocks. The Innkeeper Comes Out

God bless you, friend, we would enquire
Have you a room that we could hire?

Second Innkeeper, Servilus

What's this? Bah! Beggars, on my life,
What care I, fellow, for you and your wife?
I take in folk with money in purse,
And keep for tramps a kick and a curse.
Pack up, the pair of you. Off from my door.
Don't trouble us here with your din any more.

Mary

Sure God's own heart in ruth would melt
To see such scorn to poor folk dealt.
Need must we die of frost and fear
For certain no other lodging is near.

The Third Innkeeper, Titus, Hears Her Cries and Comes Out

What, lass? So full of tears and cries?
Come: mean you to weep out your eyes?
My house is full and it grieves me sore
That I cannot open to you my door.

24

But if you would lie in the stable here
You are welcome and more to such poor cheer.

Mary

Ah, good mine host, we stand not in mind
This night to lie soft on a goose feather bed.
We ask but a wall to ward the wind
And a roof to keep the snow from our head.

Innkeeper

Come, enter then—till it befall
My house have room—within this stall.

Joseph Sings

O maiden, here is shelter o'er thee,
Here is a cradle for thee,
Where we with God shall sleep
Who made and shall us keep.

Mary Sings

Ah, Joseph mine,
Thou must my comfort be alone:
The time draws near that I must bear
With pain and many a grievous moan
My little child, my Jesukin.

Joseph

Tomorrow with the break of day
I must be stirring and away,
In Cana market my ox to set,
And see what offers I shall get;
Then with the money back to town
Post-haste, and pay the tribute down.

Mary

A single ox will sell so dear,
Think you, to pay the tribute clear?

Joseph

Nay never doubt when I come back
No single farthing shall we lack.

Mary

Ah, Joseph, now the hour is come

To lose the burden of my womb,
Fulfilled is Gabriel's word aright
And I must bear my child this night.
Then pray you again mine host to rouse
And beg he take us in his house.

Joseph

Alas, my mind misgives me sore
We'll fare no better than before.
Yet will I knock and tirl the pin,
And beg he give us room within.

As He Prepares to go to the Inn the Child is Born, While Music is Played

Sir Titus, hearken to our plight,
A child is born to us this night,
And we all frozen in yon shed.—
Open, and give us board and bed.

Innkeeper Titus

Gladly, Old Sir, I would you please,
You and your wench, and do you ease;
But here lie four and twenty head
Packed like peas-in-pod abed,
And folk asprawl on bench and floor,—
Knock, friend, at some neighbour door.
I'm Master of this Hostelry,
And order my house in my degree.

Joseph Returns

Mary, our prayers are all denied
In stable still we must abide,
But see, for cold our babe doth cry,
Lay we him in this manger nigh,
Where crowned with hay stand ox and ass
Breathing warm breath for his solace.

Mary Sings

Ah, Joseph mine,
Why is this world so faithless grown
To spurn us out of house and hall
And leave us in a cattle stall?
Ah, Joseph mine, Ah, Joseph mine,

Reach down a sheaf of hay to spread,
And make our child a bowery bed.

Joseph Sings

Dear heart, my love and all my joy,
Bring hither now thy little boy.

Mary Sings

Ah, Joseph mine,
Help me rock our little boy,
God thereof shall give me joy,
Ah, Joseph mine, Ah, Joseph mine.

Joseph Sings

O, thou dearest Mario,
Lullay I sing, lulli lullo,
I help thee rock thy little boy,
God therefore shall give me joy,
Mario, Mario!

Mary Sings

Ah, Joseph, Mary's angel sings,
Sings Gloria for these tidings;
The Love to earth is brought
For which we strove and wrought,
Our little child, our Jesukin.

Joseph and Mary Stay By the Manger While the Company Walk Round and Sing

A child is born in Bethlehem,
    This year, this year,
Wherefore exult Jerusalem,
    This year we joy and sing.
We sing the Mother of our Lord
    And Jesus her sweet boy,
And Christ we sing above all thing
    This year with mirth and joy.

Now lies he in a manger small,
    This year, this year,
Who shall at last be Lord of all,
    This year we joy and sing,
We sing the Mother of our Lord,
    And Jesus her sweet boy,

And Christ we sing above all thing
  This year with mirth and joy.

Gallus Enters and Speaks

Ut Hoy!
What? Am I not last? I thought so to be,
Yet nor Huckle nor Muckle before me I see.
So freezing cold in face it blows
No longer can I feel my nose.
This day to Huckle, my good friend,
I, Gallus, did my two gloves lend.
Then canst thou figure in thy pate
What makes friend Huckle come so late?
I look around. Lo, clear as day
Comes Huckle, fast as Huckle may.

Huckle

Ut Hoy!
What? Am I not first? I thought to be,
But here brother Gallus before me I see.

Gallus

Huckle, how fare our flocks on the wold?

Huckle

With thy sheep, Gallus, I was right cold.

Gallus

Cold, Huckle? Of that I am full sad.
But look on my two hands, my lad.

Huckle

What, hast thou but two? Thou liest by this head:
Take here a hundred of mine in their stead.
But canst thou figure in thy pate
What makes friend Muckle come so late?
I look around. Lo, clear as day,
Comes Muckle fast as Muckle may.

Muckle

Ut Hoy!
What, am I not first? I thought so to be,
But Gallus and Huckle before me I see.

Huckle

Eh, Muckle, hast been round the world? By this
   head,
Waiting for thee we were like to be dead.

Muckle

Aye, for my good wife would not let me out,
Until I had stitched her shoes all about,
But brothers, if this frost shall keep,
Must have a care of us and sheep.

Gallus

Good Huckle, hast not heard men say
The Lord Cyrinus hath laid this day
A mighty tax on every head,
Which all must pay, in fear and dread
That all their goods shall forfeit be?
Who now shall you find from terror free?

Huckle

Eh, Gallus, what is't thou dost say?
A mighty tax that all must pay?
Is there no end to poor folk's need?
The last crumb taken of their bread?

Muckle

Great God, will taxes never bate?
Must trouble still on trouble wait?
T'is time the poor man's sweat and swink
Brought him at least his meat and drink.
A load of trouble I see in store,
And hunger stalking at every door.

Gallus

Ah, Muckle, thou hast nought to bewail,
If thou talk trouble, hear first my tale.
Sure never did shepherd such woes befall,
By night nor day I sleep not at all;
I hold such watch and ward o'er my sheep,
I scarce can tell when I last did sleep.
Yestreen was I in field with my men,
To count our sheep began we then,

29

Full short was the tale we found by our tally,—
I shall you tell how they did miscarry.

Huckle

Say on; old gibberer.

Gallus

Say part—the wicked wolf had eaten them.

Huckle

Belike the butcher's dog had bitten them.
So untoward this hap did befall—
Must the wolf bear the blame for all?

Gallus

What, must thy tongue be still a-jog?
See, the wolf can bite you as hard as the dog.

Huckle

Nay, harder, by this head.

Gallus

What further wouldst say hereof, must thou keep.
Time is it now to be watching thy sheep.

Muckle

Look you, my wife has put something up—
Turf cakes and pasties. What, shall we sup?

Huckle

And is there no hunk of dripping, man?

Muckle

Whist!
Three pieces, and each as big as your fist!

They Eat and Drink With Much Mutual Courtesy

Muckle

Late have I heard it told in some fashion,
How God from eternity on men hath compassion,
And sendeth Messiah his word to fulfil,
To redeem and to comfort men of good will;

30

The sickness of earth he shall amend,
And of all burdens shall make an end.

Gallus

Ah, were that day already here,
That unto us Messiah appear,
For joy and bliss would we leap and spring,
And shout to God in thanksgiving.
Ut Hoy!

*Here They Stand in a Triangle Resting on Their
Long Crooks. After Each Speech They Jump Into
the Air With Shouts of Joy*

Huckle

O in what hour? And in what place,
Shall he be born that brings such grace?
Ut hoy!

Muckle

The hour we may not truly tell,
But what the place we know right well.
In Bethlehem born shall he be,
And of a choice maid certainly.
Ut hoy!

Gallus

Now, brothers, be our wills agreed,
I rede you rest is shepherd's need
So on the ground let each him lay
And sleep a little till it be day.

The Shepherds Lie Down and Sleep

The Angel Sings

Gloria, Gloria in excelsis!
Joy, Shepherds, Joy and good tiding
To you and all mankind I bring.
O Shepherds, Christ wake you,
From slumber now shake you,
To Bethlem betake you,
Shepherds each one.
Run to the stable, the manger, the cradle,

31

To the young one, the Maid's son, run, Shepherds,
   run.
Haste ye, O haste ye, here lies your way,
Take pipe, take tabor, and play, Shepherds, play.
Run to Bethlem, seek out the stall,
Greet the youngling, one and all,
O you Shepherds, be not cast down,
Hark to the news that I make known.

Gallus Speaks In His Dream

Eh, Huckle, who is this so late
That thus doth sing and jubilate?
Some ghost this night has lost his way,
And leads us in our dreams astray.

Huckle

I marvel greatly what this may be.
Somewhat under my hat did I see,
When lo, a great and shining light—
What should it be?—before my sight.

Muckle

And in my ears a sound did ring.
Sure, none but angels can so sing.

The Angel Sings

From Heaven above to earth I bring
A blessed word of good tiding.
Yea, News of joy and mirth this day
To all mankind I sing and say.

Gallus Gets Up and Speaks To Muckle

Have a care, 'tis frozen over.

Muckle

Ay, blockhead, 'tis smooth as glass.
My beard is full of ice.

Gallus

Huckle, get up. The sky is cracking.

Huckle

Let it crack. It's old enough to have cracked
   before.

Gallus

Huckle, get up. The little birds are singing.

Huckle

Let 'em sing. They've got small heads; they're soon awake.

Gallus

Huckle, get up. The drivers are cracking their whips on the road.

Huckle

Let 'em crack 'em. They've far enough to go.

Gallus

Come, man, thou must get up.

He Raises Huckle, Who at Once Falls Again

Have a care, 'tis frozen over.

Huckle

Frozen it is, by this head.
Couldst not open thy mouth to say so, before I laid open my brains?

Muckle

But Gallus, good Gallus, what hast thou dreamed, that thou didst so mumble and rumble by me in thy sleep?
What hast thou dreamed then?

Gallus

What have I dreamed?
That can I well say.

Before Each Song the Shepherds Jump Round on Their Crooks so as to Face Outwards in a Triangle

Gallus Sings

As by a stall I rode this night
Of ox and ass I saw a sight,
That from a manger fed,

33

O Child most rare, O maiden fair,
That stood beside his bed.
And when I woke from slumber deep,
" 'fore God, I would a sennight sleep
For such a dream," I said.

Huckle

But Muckle, good Muckle, what hast thou
dreamed, that thou didst so mumble and rumble
by me in thy sleep?
What hast thou dreamed then?

Muckle

What have I dreamed?
That can I well say.

Muckle Sings

All in the Holy Night so still
A slumber deep upon me fell,
And soon, as I lay sleeping,
A sweetness like to honey stole
Or fragrant roses on my soul—
With joy my heart was leaping.

Gallus

But, Huckle, good Huckle, what has thou
dreamed that thou didst so mumble and rumble
by me in thy sleep?
What hast thou dreamed then?

Huckle

What have I dreamed?
That can I well say.

Huckle Sings

I dreamed, and lo an angel came
And led us unto Bethlehem,
In Judah's land so far.
And there a wondrous thing befell,
Good news, good news on earth to tell,
In heaven a shining star.

The Shepherds Sing and Dance

Lusty, trusty Shepherd boys,
That love to make a cheerful noise,
Heigh ho, foot it while you sing,
Evil fails and good doth spring.
David was a shepherd young,
David cheers both heart and tongue.

Lusty singing by our sheep,
When we have no mind to sleep;
Who to stop our mouths dare try,
Shouting praise to God most High?
Sing, lads, who shall say you nay?
David's self did sing and play.

After many a mighty stroke,
He shall raise his chosen folk,
Kings and potentates put down,
He shall wear at last the crown.
Every soul in David joys—
Are not Shepherds lusty boys?

Gallus

Have with you to Bethlem, then, say I,
To see this sight beyond compare.
Yet what should we take to one so high,
What gift can we give when we come there?

Huckle

A bottle of milk have I for this need
That mother and child alike shall feed.

Muckle

A lamb, the best my flock can yield—
Of which full worthy is such a child—
On my two shoulders will I lift,
And to that child will make my gift.

Gallus

A bundle of wool with me will I take
That his mother full soft his bed may make.

Huckle

So dark grows the night, no more can I say

Whether or no we have kept the way.
What say you, fellows, go we right?

Gallus

Huckle, I see before me a light.
There let us go and ask them fair
If God's Son haply be lodged there,
Or beg they tell us, as best they know,
Whither to find him we must go.
Hallo there. Open the door, we pray.
Shepherds we are that would ask our way.

Joseph

My friends, let one among you speak
And freely say what here you seek.
With searching looks and eager mind
You come,—what think you here to find?

Huckle

It is God's Son we would find out
That lies in a stable hereabout.
For so to us it has been revealed,
And we seek him, leaving our flocks afield.

Joseph

Come, enter then, if such your mind.
Here is the child you look to find.

The Three Shepherds Place Themselves Before Joseph and Mary and Sing

Shepherds

Behold, my heart, what thing is here,
That in the crib so sweetly lies;
It is God's Son, His pretty one,
His Child, the youngling Jesus dear.

Gallus Speaks as He Offers His Gift

Greeting to thee, child most rare,
That lies in manger cold and bare.
No feather bed hast thou this day,
Thy pallet the spiky straw and hay.
Thou camest not with summer's rose
But with the winter's ice and snows,

And for thy lily thou must see
White fields of frost encompass thee.
Ah, youngling, pity it is to behold
Thy little cheeks so pinched with cold,
To see thy pretty golden eyes
Weep bitter tears, to hear thy cries.
Look, little one, take this wool for thy bed,
Whereon thou softly mayest rest thy head.
I bring thee, too, some meal to bake
That thy Mother may make thee therewith a cake,
And if again I come by the door
Thou shalt not fail of presents more.

Huckle Speaks as He Offers His Gift

Greeting to thee, child most rare,
All stiff with cold thou liest there.
In Heaven thou hadst a mansion great,
Yet cold and naked is here thy state.
Take thou this milk to stay thy weeping
Whereby I give me to thy keeping.

Muckle Speaks as He Offers His Gift

Greeting to thee, child most sweet,
Yea, little Jesus, God thee greet.
In cattle stall thou, King, dost rest,
Thy mother giveth thee her breast.
I bring thee, King, this lambkin white
Wherein thou mayest much delight.

Joseph

Shepherds I thank you that you bring
Your gifts and worthy offering.

Mary Sings

Shepherds, I thank you that you bring
Your gifts and worthy offering.
God grant you sustenance, and keep
And bless from every harm your sheep.

The Shepherds Sing

Before the crib we kneel
And him we rock and swing,
The child that shall us heal,

37

And to him blessing bring,
Sweet Jesukin, sweet Jesukin.

The Shepherds Go Away From the Crib

Gallus

Eh, lads, how is't befallen thus
That he is born where none could guess?
In such poor place to see the day
Who doth the whole world rule and sway?

Muckle

On earth is he born in this poor fashion
So that on us he have compassion,
And make us rich in Heaven great
That like to angels shall be our state.
Yea, poorly is he born this day
That so from pride men turn them away,
And choose not riches and glorification,
But to live content in humble station.

Huckle

Now may we be of courage good
That he is born of kingly blood.
King David was a shepherd bred—
In holy writ so have I read—
That all alone with might and main
Goliath, that dread giant, hath slain.

Gallus

But when we to our fellows tell
The sight that here to us befell,
They'll not believe what we report,
But will of us make mock and sport,
In such strange fashion is this bestead
It much may rack the wisest head.

Muckle

It were great peril that this be unknown;
Forthwith to the gentry it must be shown.
Tomorrow to Jerusalem will I repair
And tell it likewise to the Mayor.

The Shepherds Sing and Dance

38

Lusty, trusty shepherd boys,
That love to make a cheerful noise,
Heigh ho, foot it while you sing,
Evil fails and good doth spring.
David was a shepherd young,
David cheers both heart and tongue.

Huckle

See, Crispin, good Crispin cometh this way,
Who hath sought us without our yea or nay.
God give you good morrow, Crispin.

Crispin

I thank you in God's name, old friend.

Gallus

How goes it with our sheep, Crispin?

Crispin

Truly, the sheep in shippon do bide,
Both the big and the little by their side;
But, brothers, what news have ye found out?
Is it true what makes such stir hereabout?

Gallus

Truly in Bethlem that child most high
Twixt ox and ass we saw him lie:
And wouldst thyself behold this sight,
Thou mayest rise with morning light
And with us to Bethlem journey aright

Crispin

Is it far to go?

Gallus

Till thou comest there!

Crispin

Must think upon that child. Mayhap
Shall get a tassel from my cap!

The Shepherds Sing, and Dance

Thus the Shepherds merrily
Their flocks and herds were keeping,

Meat they took, and down they lay
All together sleeping.
To them an Angel did appear,
And God shone about them clear,
That they were sore amazed.
The Angel spake 'Fear you nothing,
Good news to all mankind I bring,
With joy your hearts be raised'.

The Company Sing

Let all mankind rejoice this morn,
Both rich and poor be glad,
For unto us a child is born,
And all things hath he made.
A Holy Child this same,
And Jesus Christ his name,
Who all for sinful man's misdeeds
To earth from Heaven came.

O Man, bethink you how this child,
Of earth nothing afraid,
In Bethlem born of maiden mild
Was in a stable laid;
Was laid in manger low,
As Holy writ doth show,
Who is the King of all the World
Both now and evermore.

The Angel Speaks

Most reverent Worships, both Master and Dame,
Our service. To you, pretty maidens, the same,
I come but to say, now all is ended,
We trust there are none that we have offended.
So think no evil nor chide our play,
But if in aught we have gone astray,
And shown your Worships what was not fit,
Blame not our will, but our lack of wit.
Show we have pleased, so all's made right—
And we wish you from God Almighty, Good
   Night.

*　　*　　*

THE THREE KINGS' PLAY

The Company Sing

Bless, O Lord, thy way we tread,
Bless our coming and our going:
Bless likewise our daily bread,
Bless our leaving and our doing.
Bless our death with thy death's leaven
That to us thy life be given.

The Angel Speaks

In right good faith I enter this place.
God give you good evening of his grace,
A right good evening, the best of cheer,
The Lord of Heaven grant each man here.
Most reverent Worships, both Master and Dame,
Our service. To you, pretty maidens, the same.
Pray do not grudge or grouch this day
For one brief hour to hear our play.
We bring you here no Heathen tale,
Nor things men gossip o'er their ale,
Which for your Worships were all unfit,
But all is ta'en from Holy Writ,
Namely of the Wise Men three;
High in the East a Star they see,
Wherefore a Journey far they go,
As every wiseman's son doth know.
At Jerusalem their steps are stayed,
To seek that child out and that Maid;
Whereat Lord Herod, waxen wroth,
Chargeth his High Priests, by their troth,
To search with haste the Scriptures through,
And of their prophecy tell him true.
So would you hear us with good heed,
Sit still, and speak no more than need.

The Page Places the Throne in Position. King Melchior Seats Himself and Speaks

Go, Boy, fetch hither my compass and chart,
My globe, and the instruments of mine art;
This star to study will I essay
That shone not in Heaven before this day—

41

When Venus with the Sun is conjoined
It augers something new to my mind.

The Page Fetches an Optic Tube

A dazzling brightness meets my gaze—
This star doth fill me with amaze.
So fair a light must needs presage
Some holy thing unto our age.
Right in the middle a maid I see
That bears a child upon her knee.
Her forehead, shining clear and bright,
Outdoes that star and pales its light.
But see, it moves, it mounts on high,
Swifter and swifter athwart the sky.
The child upon that maiden's breast
Turns himself unto the East.
Go, Boy, fetch hither our mathematician,
To cast this star in its position.
It were much wisdom to unfold
What mean this maid and child of old.

The Page Speaks

Most noble King, I hear and obey
And will fetch Viligratia hither straightway.

Enter Viligratia

King Melchior Speaks

This star, what canst thou tell of it?

Viligratia Speaks

Nothing, O King, of mine own wit
But if the prophets we read aright
Great mysteries are brought to light;
As that Esaias hath foretold
Now I bethink me of prophets old,
'In Bethlehem shall a maid give birth,
And her child, the King of Heaven and Earth.'

King Melchior Speaks

Surely that thing the prophet said,
In Bethlehem now is compassed;
Wherefore much vexed am I to know
What gift on him I may bestow.

A heap of gold I think to bring,
For gold is worthiest of a king,
That shall both Heaven and Earth inherit;
I trust thereby his grace to merit.
Page, within this hour we part,
Go, make all ready for the start.
Viligratia, as our regent reign
Till to our realm we come again.

Viligratia Speaks

Most gracious King, an't be thy will,
I shall this office high fulfil.

They Go Out. The Page Rearranges the Throne.
King Balthazzar Seats Himself and Speaks

What's this they tell me, that this night
Great mysteries are come to light?
Namely, a star most bright and clear
Wherein a maiden doth appear,
All with a King of earth and heaven,
A tender child, both young and fair,
A child most wonderful, most rare,—
To him must incense needs be given.
This star, this child, this king to greet
Now step I out into the street.
Pray, is this thing to others known
That unto me my folk have shown?
O wonder, the like I ne'er heard tell
In saga nor in chronicle.
Maid and Mother was none I guess,
Nor child king, rich yet penniless.
To Bethlehem beckons us this star,—
Then follow, though the way be far.
I know not well on learned ground
This mystery's thesis to expound:—
A child that lieth in a stall
Shall be the King of Jewry all.
Wherefore with daybreak let me rise,
And find that child out where he lies.

He Goes Out. The Page Again Prepares the Throne.
King Caspar Speaks

O wonder rare, O highest bliss,
The very time fulfilled is

43

That born should be Messiah child
And of a maiden undefiled.
See, the star doth call us hence
Homage to do, and reverence,
And throughly maketh us to know
All the prophets did foreshow.
With brightest beams it becks us on
To find that Mother and that Son.
Since he is King of Heaven and Earth
Myrrh must be offered for his birth.
With such oblation to commend me
I trust to win him to befriend me.

He Goes Out. The Page Removes the Throne.
The Company Sing

Shine star and light the Wisemen's way,
The king of Heaven and Earth this day
Is to our world descended.
And wise men seeking for a king
Where learnt ye this last secret thing,
Whence came this wisdom splendid?
Follow, follow
From lands afar,
O'er hill and hollow
Follow the star
To the stall where the child is tended.

King Melchior Enters With Page. The Page Speaks

Most gracious king, a noise I hear,
A rout of folk is riding near.
Meseems that on a King they stay
Who freely will direct our way.

King Melchior Speaks

Withdraw, and leave me here alone
While to these strangers I make me known.

The Page Goes Off

Greetings, good friends, pray whither bound
With such stout hearts, thus richly found?

King Balthazzar Speaks

Our loves to you Sir: but whither go ye
And all your noble company?

44

King Melchior Speaks

We thank your loves, and do intend
To Jerusalem our journey's end.

King Caspar Speaks

To that same city we too repair,
Then tell us, pray, what make you there?

King Melchior Speaks

'Tis clear to read in Esaiay
A child shall be upon a day,
In Bethlehem shall be his birth
That is the King of Heaven and Earth.
But now a marvel is to learn—
So bright a star in Heaven doth burn,
That, wot you well, this very morn,
That child and king is surely born.

King Balthazzar Speaks

Of very truth I may you tell
To us that self-same thing befell.
A star before our gaze shone clear
Wherein did maid and child appear.
Surely this day hath brought to light
What heathen times long hid from sight.

King Caspar Speaks

Sirs, this is fallen in marvellous sort,
Me, too, this star hath hither brought.
To find that child is all our passion,—
Then must we stir in busy fashion.

King Melchior Speaks

The star doth like a beacon shine
Riding before us for a sign.
Yet nothing of the road we know
And must no means of help forego.
Friends, since in such a case we stand,
Strangers here in a strange land,
I counsel that we turn aside
And to Jerusalem city ride,
These tidings there to noise abroad
And seek for guidance on our road.

They Sing

Three Kings a-leading and what led them?
A star that stood o'er Bethlehem,
Over a stable
And over a cradle.

The Company Sing

Three wise men in King Herod's days
From Eastern lands they took their ways.

As to Jerusalem they came
The Christ was born in Bethlehem.

Then asked they of low and high
Where that newborn King should lie,

Among the Jews by prophets old
Clearly unto us foretold.

The Devil Places Herod's Throne in Position.

King Herod Enters With His Lackey and Speaks

I am the King of all this land.
God help me if I slack my hand!
Acclaimed by my people all
Lord spiritual and temporal,
Acknowleged by the Jewish moot
Omnipotent King, Lord absolute.
This day a judgement seat I hold
Wherein I judge both young and old,
They throng in crowds our council room
To see our state and hear their doom.
So, let them grovel on the floor—
Who's that who knocks upon the door?

The Lackey Speaks

Most gracious King, here is a press,
Twere hard to know their business.
Much Lords and Kings are in their throng,
In splendid garb they pace along,
Majestic in their port. God send
They come not here for evil end.

King Herod Speaks

Go, ask of them what is their mind
And what from us they look to find.

46

The Lackey Speaks to King Melchior

King Herod greets your Lordships well;
Of your intent he would hear tell,
What blood ye are, and from what land,
And what ye look for at his hand.

King Melchior Answers

Of kingly stem we all are born,
Two are from Saba, the third from Morn,
King Herod's self we fain would greet,
And with his favour trust to meet.

The Lackey Returns and Speaks to Herod

Of kingly stem they all are born,
Two are from Saba, the third from Morn,
King Herod's self they fain would greet,
And with his favour trust to meet.

King Herod Speaks

Escort them hither. We are at leisure,
And grant them audience at our pleasure.

The Lackey Speaks to the Three Kings

The King your presence doth beseech,
And with your Lordships would fain have speech.

The Three Kings Come Before Herod, Who Speaks

Welcome, my lords. What would ye of me,
That hither you ride from far country?

King Caspar Speaks

Your Kingly love we fain would win
To hear our journey's origin.
In Saba, in our land afar,
Rose in the East a wondrous star,
Wherein a maid a child did bear,—
Mark well, O King, what you do hear;
Whereat we marvelled much with mirth,
And said, Messiah is born on earth.
A child he shall hold kingly sway
And all the Jews shall him obey.
Him now to seek with eager care,
Unto your court, O king, we fare.

47

Herod Speaks

What? In my land can such things be,
And known to strangers and not to me?
Sirs, get you gone to Bethlem straight,
And find that child and King algate,
And when ye have done him reverence
And offered gifts in his presence,
Return, and hither tidings bring—
We too would take an offering;
A kingly gift we shall devise.
This do with speed and enterprise,
And win much favour in our eyes.

King Caspar Speaks

Great King, fear not to find us slack
To bring hot-haste our tidings back.

King Melchior Speaks

To horse! To horse!
To Bethlehem take we now our course.

King Balthazzar Speaks

See, it moves athwart the sky,
The star that erst we did espy,
In our eastern land aglow,
Whereby that child we first 'gan know.

The Angel Leads the Kings Out

King Herod Speaks

This news doth move me to fear and anger,
Being no true King here but a stranger.
Go, lackey, fetch some learned priest,
I will ask him of this star in the East,
This King the Jews must needs obey—
Go, fetch a High Priest here straightway.

The Lackey Speaks

Most gracious King, I hear and obey,
Instanter will I ride away,
From every corner of the land
To fetch a High Priest to your hand.

He Brings the Priests To Herod. Caiaphas Speaks

Lord Herod, Caiaphas am I,

48

Would never give my King the lie;
But I must say you such a thing,
Such a thing, my sweetest king,
An if your Majesty will promise
To bear poor Caiaphas no malice.

Herod Speaks

Say on, Sir, nor our anger fear,
Though little pleasure 'tis to hear;
Nor will we not our malice wreak,
Seeing we called you here to speak,
But if of prophecy ought you would
See that it be of omen good.

Caiaphas, Pilate and Jonas Speak Together, Very Quickly and Excitedly

Great King, this speak I in your ear.
Thus the psalmist singeth clear:
David's son shall think no scorn
In Judah's Bethlem to be born,
His sons shall swallow up his foes,
And vanquish all who him oppose.
Much folk shall follow him on earth
And be blessed in his birth.
His name shall be Emmanuel
So prophesieth Ezekiel,
Butter and honey shall he eat,
Good and right he shall entreat,
But evil set beneath his feet.

Herod Speaks

But how may be a thing so rare
As that a maid a child should bear?

Caiaphas Speaks

The seed of the woman shall bruise the serpent's
    head,
What was lost he shall find, and his life shall
    quicken the dead.

Herod Speaks

A neighbour King hath sought me out,
And counselled me beyond a doubt,
And said: In Bethlehem this morn

49

A Saviour to the world is born.
A righteous prince, a shepherd true,
That all men give him homage due.
O King, said he, stop not thine ear
But ponder well what thou dost hear.
If this be true, 'twere plain to see
My crown stands much in jeopardy.

Caiaphas Speaks

O Sire, it were a pretty tale
To think (ha ha!) your realm should fail!
A King he shall be called, pardy,
But wield less power than a flea.
Condemned to die a death of shame,
All men shall curse his people's name.

Herod Speaks

Methinks it were the better way
While still he is young to put him away.

Pilate Speaks

Sweet Sovereign, set your mind at ease
Nor let this bubble fret your peace,
Until the wise men homeward bound
Say truly whether thus 'twas found.

Herod Speaks

Much fear we lest these tidings ride
Already through the countryside,
For yester e'en (so were we told)
While Shepherds watched upon the wold
Sudden an Angel them beforn
Proclaimed a King was newly born.
Sir Caiaphas, say, upon what ground
Shall this new born King be found
To whom the Jews shall do service?
What can your prophets tell of this?

Jonas Speaks

All prophets with one voice maintain
Christ the King is without stain,
In Bethlehem he shall be born
That lieth in Judea's land,
Thereto all prophets do set their hand.

Herod Speaks

Right!
Enough and plenty for tonight!
Be off, and make of this no chatter,
Myself will undertake this matter.

The Lackey Drives the Priests Away

I'll work my wits, I'll stir about,
I'll let the young knave's blood out!
Ah! how the devil laughs this day
To see me cast my soul away.
What? must King Herod plead and cry?
Far better curse my fate and die.
What other can I do or say?
Will no one be my help this day?
Robbed of my throne, bereft of friend,
I wait my miserable end.
Will no one do poor Herod right?
No God? No man? No Fiend? No Sprite?
But out, alas, of all forsook,
Whither for friendship can I look?
O woe! O woe!

The Devil Springs in Lustily and Speaks to Herod

O Ho, O Ho,
What make you here with moan and groan?
Here's one leaves not his friends alone.
Say on, what is this direful need?

Herod Speaks

For very fear I die indeed
That in Judea a King is born,
And I, of every friend forlorn.
Ah me, poor devil, what shall I do?

The Devil Speaks

Peace, peace, I am a devil too,
And devil must by devil stand.
Pluck up your courage, man. My hand
To see you safely through this thing.
Together we will have this King.
Trust me to counsel what's to do,
I am no more his friend than you.
Arm, King, and strike—Make no delay.

Herod Speaks

So many, partner, must I slay?
Not one alone, but score on score?
For my own skin I tremble sore.
For such an evil, alack! alack!
In my own coin they'll pay me back.
I fear for this they'll see me dead.

The Devil Speaks

Pish! put this nonsense from your head.
What, would you be a devil, Sir King?
Hark now, I have the very thing.
All little childer of two year old,
Or under, get them in your hold—
Child or Mother you shall spare none,
Born or unborn, all is one—
And when you've got them in your noose,
Ha! how the fox will maul the goose!
My cronies must not miss this joke!
Presto! in a puff of smoke,
Rag and bag, goes old Nick Nack
To fetch his fellows on his back!

Herod and the Devil Go Out. The Company Sing

With God we fain would tune our song again.
While Herod now doth arm his hand,
Onward the three Kings ride.
The star that is their guide
O'er Bethlehem stays, and still doth stand.

The Three Kings Sing

A Child is born in Bethlehem,
    This year, this year,
Wherefore exult Jerusalem,
    This year we joy and sing.
We sing the Mother of our Lord,
    And Jesus her sweet boy,
And Christ we sing above all thing
    This year with mirth and joy.

Now lies he in a manger small,
    This year, this year,
Who shall at last be Lord of all,
    This year we joy and sing.

We sing the Mother of our Lord,
    And Jesus her sweet boy,
And Christ we sing above all thing
    This year with mirth and joy.

King Caspar Speaks

O Lord, I pray,
Forsake us not,
Lighten our eyes in this great need,
That we die not the death. O lead,
Lead us, Lord, the narrow way
That we stumble not, nor stray,
But walk as ever in thy light.

King Melchior Speaks

Here are two ways, which is the right?

King Balthazzar Speaks

See, see, the star doth stop and stay,
To yonder stall make we our way.
God greet you, maiden without peer,
Surely the child we seek lies here?

Mary Sings

The child ye seek ye have surely found
In swaddling clothes all meanly bound.

King Melchior Speaks

Come then,
Our gifts to offer make we bold
Myrrh, frankincense and the red red gold.

*The Page Takes Their Sceptres From the Kings,
and Brings Them Their Gifts With Much Ceremony*

King Melchior Sings

Psallite unigenito
Christo, dei filio,
Psallite redemptori
Domino puerulo
Jacenti in praesepio.

The Kings Sing

Now which of us shall be the first?

53

King Caspar Speaks

Sir, you are eldest here, I wis,
Wherefore to you this honour is.
Enter, and we will come behind,
So seems it best unto my mind.

King Balthazzar Speaks

The honour is yours, Sir, by kingly use.

King Melchior Speaks

I will this honour not refuse.
In God's name, then, I enter here,
And to this child I bring new year.

King Melchior Kneels Before Mary and Makes His Offering

Blest be thou, child, and blest thy dame,
And blest be God I hither came.
A journey far we needs have made
To find this place where thou are laid,
I pray thee, and I give this gold,
That for thy friend thou wilt me hold.
Friends, treat this child with honour due,
And rear ye him as parents true.
Nothing for tears hast thou, sweet boy,
And of my gifts I wish thee joy.

King Caspar's Offering

All hail, great King and Hero great,
Though meanly here thou keep'st thy state.
Here have we sought thee in a shed—
Not so a king should make his bed.
A star hath hither been my guide,
O king, and homeward when I ride
Each hour, I'll think upon thee, yea,
Thy praise be in my mouth alway
Till all the world shall know thy worth.—
Take here this sweetness of the earth,
Myrrh, gathered in my eastern land,
Whereby I give me to thy hand.

King Balthazzar's Offering

Now come I too, Thou Kingly Grace,

Thou Hero, born of royal race,
For thee with heart and soul I yearn,
Before my steps thy star did burn.
This incense for my gift I bring,
Which well befits one born a king.
Sire, if hereafter I come to thee,
I pray receive me graciously.

Joseph Speaks

Most worthy Sirs, God give you meed,
That sought us out and in sore need
With gifts did comfort our poor state;
In Heaven your reward is great.

Mary Sings

Sirs, for your gifts and love this day,
Our love and thanks be yours alway,
Be blest in what this night has showed,
And with fresh courage take your road.

King Caspar Speaks

Now farewell, Joseph, goodman friend,
Be zealous still this child to tend,
For him nor toil or trouble spare;
The Lord himself reward your care.

King Balthazzar Speaks

Now God, the everlasting Lord,
From fear and danger be thy ward.

King Melchior Speaks

To Herod next our steps are bound
To tell him where this child is found—
But Sirs, the darkness falls apace,
Needs must we couch us in this place.

The Three Kings Leave. They Sing and Fall Asleep

Upon a night I lay and slept.

The Angel Enters Before the Kings and Speaks

You holy kings from Orient,
Of God Almighty am I sent
That unto you I should reveal
Great peril treadeth at your heel.

55

Get you not home the selfsame way
Lest Herod shall you take and slay,
Who secretly doth hide his wrath;
God shall you show another path.

King Melchior Speaks

A marvellous dream here have I heard.
An angel stayed me with a word,
That Herod's house we should pass by
And home another way should hie,
For in his raging he hath sworn
To do to death this child new-born.

King Balthazzar Speaks

That selfsame dream I too have dreamed;
An angel warned us, so meseemed,
That Herod worketh wit and will,
The lifeblood of this child to spill—
But, an thou plann'st this devilry,
Herod, thou gett'st no help from me.

The Kings Sing as They Go Out

Balthazzar King rides over the hill,
He hath found the child and wrought his will,
Hath wrought, hath wrought his will.

The Angel Enters and Speaks to Joseph

Joseph, Joseph, mark you well,
Good soul, the word I shall you tell
From God who hath me hither sped.
Rise, Joseph, make not here your bed,
Rise, man, take wife and child by hand
And get you straight to Egypt's land,
Nor to Judea back return
Till of this matter more you learn.

Joseph Speaks

And must we fare abroad this night?
Ah, grievous, grievous is our plight—
To Egypt's land how shall we go
When nothing of the road we know,
While savage beasts beset the way
And prowling robbers stalk their prey,
And 'tis a mighty way to ride?

56

Mary Sings

God will surely be our guide
And lead us rightly on the way,
Nor suffer his own folk to stray.
His angel with us He will send
And bring us surely to the end.
Come then, make ready with good heart,
Saddle the ass, 'tis time to part.

Joseph Speaks

Dear House, God have thee in his care,
I shall not find thy like elsewhere.
But 'tis God's will I should thee leave,
His first commandment to achieve.

Mary Sings

Farewell, we may not more abide,
To Egypt's land we needs must ride.

(They Go Off)

King Herod Enters With His Attendants and Speaks

What though I plotted had and planned,
And with my sly and cunning hand
Made ready a right royal feast
To greet these kings from out the East,
And this Sir Child they do revere,
Yet in my bones I have a fear
They did beguile me and betray
And robbed poor Herod of his prey.
I think and think and think again
How best to set this thing in train,
And when I have him in my net
What gift from me 'twere best he get.
Full subtly will I go to work,
Like fox that in the hedge doth lurk,
While all his heart and sense is set
Some fat goose in his maw to get.
As crafty as a cat i' the house
I'll be, that hears a wainscot mouse.
And now I have it, by good hap,
A plan this infant to entrap,—
With my all-conquering warrior band
All babes I'll get into my hand,

Yea, all small childer in Juda's land.
And though their mothers 'murder' cry
And scream the sky down, what care I?—
So that my realm I do maintain
And my inheritance remain.

Mary Comes in a Vision Before Herod and Sings

Great king, to Mercy mend your mind
Lest grief come suddenly behind;
If so much guiltless blood you shed,
What call you, King, on your own head?

Herod Speaks

Out of my sight, thou prating witch,
What! thinkest thou a king to teach?
I tell thee, I lose both life and crown,
If not this wickedness be put down.
It were no monarch, but a hind
Would let a scold's tongue rule his mind.

To his Captain

Sir Knave! you have your orders plain,
What each must do, you and your train.
Take then our royal decree, whereto
We set our sign and seal. This do
And publish it in every town.
Take it, Sir, cry it up and down,
By village cross, in market square,
'Whereas King Herod'—cry it fair,—
'And who fulfils not these commands
Shall forfeit life and goods and lands!'

The Captain Proclaims the Decree

Let all take notice of this decree.
Whereas his puissant majesty
King Herod, our rightful sovereign lord,
Hath given order that by the sword
All little children of two year old
Or under we bring them to his hold,
Be it known, sans favour and sans fear,
None shall escape for gold nor gear,
And who fulfils not these commands
Shall forfeit life and goods and lands.

Judas Comes to Herod and Speaks

Woe's me, the cruel bloody deed!
Certes to thee our lives are feed.
But must our pretty babes be slain?
Nought comes of this but grief and pain.

Herod Speaks

The guilt of this shall rest on thee.
Go, put him under lock and key.

The Captain Speaks to Judas

Thou villain, wouldst revile the king?
I tell thee for this thou'lt surely swing.
Far better a few young children slain,
Than all of us dead like rats in a drain.

Herod Speaks

Run lackey, run with cry and hue,
Bring me my trusty captain true.
Look you, Captain, you have your sword—
Four thousand men attend your word—
Out with them, harry house and hall,
And strangle me all young children small.
On pain of death no bribe receive,
Nor pity move thee, one child to leave.
Slaughter them, every mother's son,
No rest till all to death be done.
For this henceforth draw double pay
In coin of gold of good assay.

The Captain Speaks

All it has pleased my gracious Sire
To vouchsafe to his servant's ear,
(Though all unworthy) with joy I heard
Nor failed to comprehend each word,
And will fulfil in every part
With all the sinews of my heart.
Ha, would they were already here,
Those little childer of two year!
My trusty sword would not be long
To make them sing a merry song.
My heart leaps up, I laugh, I shout,
To see the red blood gushing out,

I carol, as for some holy feast
Where men kill many a goodly beast.
Forward! thus march I to the town
To put this foul rebellion down.
Long live King Herod! Lackey, run,
And see with me this work begun.

The Lackey Speaks

With all my strength I'll hew and hack,
In work like this I'll not be slack.

The Captain Speaks

Ha! such I seek, good men and true,
To quit themselves as men should do!
Lord King, be still of courage stout,
We'll make the children's blood gush out.

Here is a Pause, and the Lights Are Darkened

The Captain Returns and Speaks

Most puissant Sire, give gracious heed
And hearken to thy servant's deed.
I with my single hand have slain
One hundred thousand, twenty and twain.
So be you still of courage stout—
We've made the children's blood gush out.

A Soldier Enters and Speaks

Eighty thousand is my sum
That I have sent to kingdom come.
The last small brat I plucked from bed,
And 'here comes a chopper' I chuckled and said—
Then out with my sword and chopped off his head.

The Lackey Speaks

Most gracious King, now be it said
What I this day have compassed.
Two thousand have I put to rest,
And hushed them at their mothers' breast.

King Herod Speaks

My thanks, good knaves. For this deed's sake
One half of my realm and riches take.

The Devil Speaks

More company, King, here's Nick come back,
And brought his children in a sack.
Curse them, young devils—if you please,
They've picked my pockets and filched the cheese.
But they shan't have bread—not a scrap of the
    worst,
Curse them, I'll see them in—Heaven first.

The Captain Speaks

Most gracious Majesty, be it known
We have searched the city up and down,
And scanned and scoured the countryside,
Hour by hour, both far and wide;
Yet search you may both high and low,
Of new born King there's nought to show;
But all small childer of years twain
At thy behest we them have slain.
Thy servants wrought what thou hast willed,
And in this hour it stands fulfilled.

Herod Speaks

Not found? Not found? Then by this hand
The felon child is fled the land.
Now dead am I, with anguish torn,
To think another God is born,—
I'll find him out, what e'er befall,
Were it at Bethlem in a stall.
Aye me, my spirit faints this day,
And all my life blood ebbs away.

The Lackey Speaks

Bring here an apple and a knife,
With sweets to stay my dear lord's life.

Angel Comes Before Herod and Sings

Herod, Herod, cruel king,
Thou hast done what wicked thing!
For thou didst the children slay,
Death shall throw at thee this day.

Herod Speaks

A cloud of light. What can it mean?

A plot against my life, I ween.
Run, lackey, run, with cry and hue
Bring me my trusty captain true.

He Comes

Look you, Captain, this sceptre take
Whereby my promised gift I make,
It hath confounded me all my day
Whereby the devil hath led me astray,
For this to Abraham's garden I fare.

Angel Speaks

Ye devils, lead him to your lair;
Long time on earth he hath served you well—
Take him home to your nest in Hell,
Wrap him in robes of royal red,
And set Hell's crown upon his head.

Captain, Lackey and the Soldiers Speak Together

What helps the sceptre now
Or crown upon the brow?
Sceptre and crown and sway
All have at last their day.

Devil Comes and Speaks

Down, Sir, down.
What hast so soon devoured the fat,
And left thy vomit on the mat?

Herod Speaks

O devil, let me longer live
And a pair of black oxen I will thee give.

Devil Speaks

None of them,
I will have thee.

Herod Speaks

O devil, let me longer live
And a pair of black horses I will thee give.

Devil Speaks

None of them,
I will have thee.

Herod Speaks

O devil, let me longer live
And half my kingdom I will thee give.

Devil Speaks

What need we bandy wordes moe?
Are not mine, come weal, come woe?
With me must dwell
In pains of hell—
And some others as well.
Wait, I will see how heavy thou art.
I harness a pair of rats,
I harness a pair of cats,
I harness a pair of mice,—
Ride, devil, ride.

He Goes Off With Herod

Captain Speaks

Ah me, what hath my lord king done,
To have slain so many a mother's son?
Ah, had I kept myself in heed,
My hand had never touched this deed.
Had I this hour my will and power
I'd hang me on the highest tree.
Had I my power and will this hour,
I'd drown me in the deepest sea,
Yet I'll revenge me on my lord,
And in my heart I plunge this sword.

Company Sing

Sing, World, and shout aloud for mirth,
Jesus, Rex, Messiah,
He the King of Heaven and earth,
Natus ex Maria.
Ox and ass the whole night through
By the Saviour stamp and chew.
Sing merry, sing wild,
Sing broad, sing fine,
Little child,
Thou art mine,
I am thine.
Shouting, singing, leaping, springing,
Hodie, Hodie,

Christ we say is born this day,
Mariae, Mariae,
He with his joy
All our annoy
Away hath ta'en
All woe, all pain.
Then make us free
To come to thee,
O Christe, O Christe.

The Angel Speaks

Most reverent Worships, both Master and Dame,
Our service. To you, pretty maidens, the same.
I come but to say, now all is ended,
We trust there are none we have offended.
So think no evil, nor chide our play,
But if in aught we have gone astray,
And shown your Worships what was not fit,
Blame not our will, but our lack of wit.
Show we have pleased, so all's made right—
And we wish you from God Almighty, Good Night.

*　　*　　*